IN MEMORY OF:

BURGESS HU

THE BULL SHARK

By Sara Green

BELLWETHER MEDIA • MINNEAPOLIS, MN

Jump into the cockpit and take flight with Pilot books. Your journey will take you on high-energy adventures as you learn about all that is wild, weird, fascinating, and fun!

This edition first published in 2013 by Bellwether Media, Inc.

No part of this publication may be reproduced in whole or in part without written permission of the publisher. For information regarding permission, write to Bellwether Media, Inc., Attention: Permissions Department, 5357 Penn Avenue South, Minneapolis, MN 55419.

Library of Congress Cataloging-in-Publication Data

Green, Sara, 1964-
 The bull shark / by Sara Green.
   pages cm. – (Pilot. Shark fact files)
 Summary: "Engaging images accompany information about the bull shark. The combination of high-interest subject matter and narrative text is intended for students in grades 3 through 7"– Provided by publisher.
 Includes bibliographical references and index.
 ISBN 978-1-60014-868-2 (hardcover : alk. paper)
 1. Bull shark–Juvenile literature. I. Title.
 QL638.95.C3G743 2013
 597.3'4–dc23
                        2012030500

Printed in the United States of America, North Mankato, MN.

TABLE OF CONTENTS

BULL SHARK
IDENTIFIED

Shallow waters off the Florida coast invite a group of swimmers on a hot day. One boy jumps off a dock into waist-deep surf to cool down. Suddenly, something bumps his leg and nearly knocks him over. Swimming near the ocean floor is a stocky gray shark with long pectoral fins. It is a bull shark, one of the most dangerous sharks in the world! The shark comes around again, this time to attack. The boy scrambles onto the dock and escapes the shark's deadly jaws with only moments to spare.

Bull sharks live in the Atlantic, Pacific, and Indian Oceans. They often hunt for prey in warm, shallow waters near coastlines. They prefer to swim in water less than 100 feet (30 meters) deep, but they will swim to depths of 490 feet (150 meters).

The bull shark is one of the few types of sharks that can live in freshwater. Bull sharks have been found in rivers around the world, including the Amazon and the Mississippi. They will even enter lakes. Bull sharks have been spotted in Central America's Lake Nicaragua and Louisiana's Lake Pontchartrain.

N

W   E   ☐ = bull shark territory

S

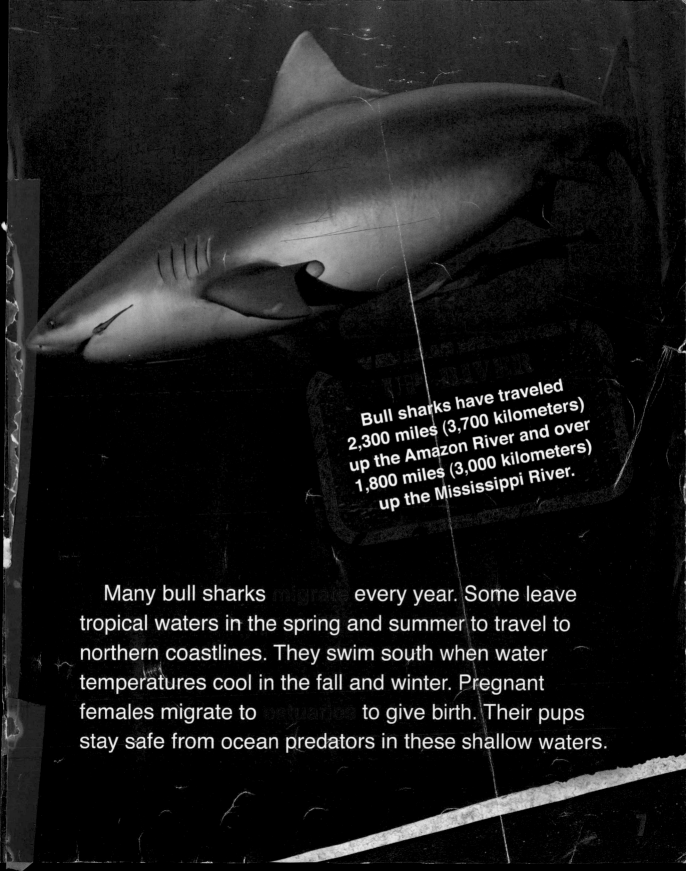

Bull sharks have traveled 2,300 miles (3,700 kilometers) up the Amazon River and over 1,800 miles (3,000 kilometers) up the Mississippi River.

Many bull sharks migrate every year. Some leave tropical waters in the spring and summer to travel to northern coastlines. They swim south when water temperatures cool in the fall and winter. Pregnant females migrate to estuaries to give birth. Their pups stay safe from ocean predators in these shallow waters.

The bull shark is known for its stout body and wide head. It can measure more than 11 feet (3.4 meters) long and weigh as much as 500 pounds (230 kilograms). However, most bull sharks are between 7 and 8 feet (2.1 and 2.4 meters) long and weigh less than 300 pounds (135 kilograms). Females are usually larger than males.

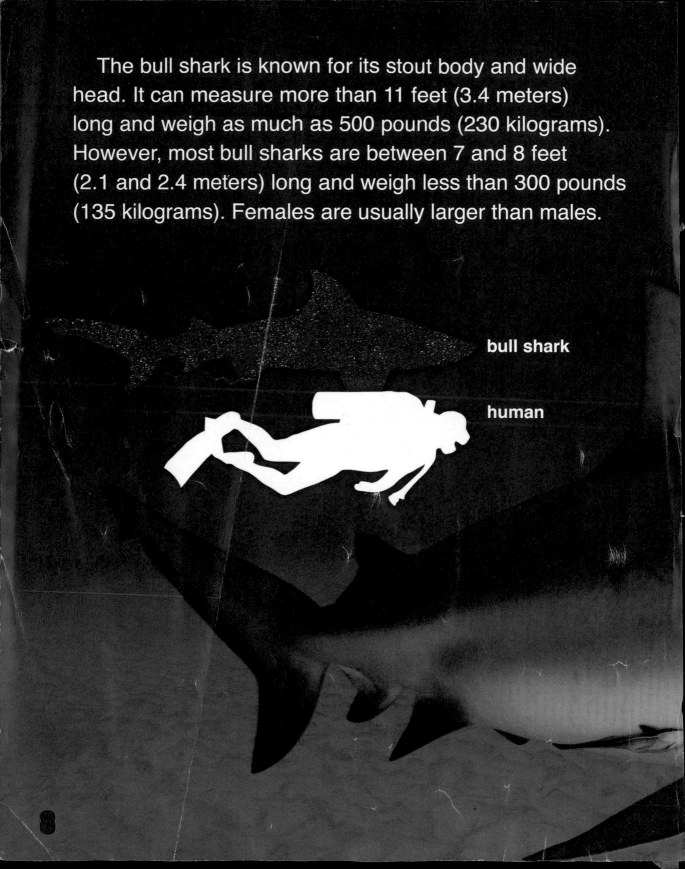

bull shark

human

The bull shark's skeleton is made of cartilage. This tissue is lighter than bone and allows the shark to move and bend with ease. The bull shark's pectoral fins help it steer. Two dorsal fins keep it balanced. A powerful tail fin propels the shark forward.

The bull shark's coloring provides camouflage. Its dark back and white belly blend in with the colors of the ocean. This countershading allows it to sneak up on prey.

Bull sharks are named for their short, blunt snouts and aggressive nature. They often butt prey with their heads before attacking. This is known as the "bump and bite."

Bull sharks are vivlparous. This means the sharks develop inside the mother's body. After 10 to 11 months, the mother gives birth to a litter of 1 to 13 pups. Newborn pups are around 29 inches (74 centimeters) long and have black fin tips that will fade with age. They are ready to swim and hunt on their own.

Bull sharks mature more slowly than other types of fish. They can reproduce when they are around 9 years old. Female bull sharks live about 16 years, and males live about 12 years.

Bull sharks are apex predators. Their strong jaws and serrated teeth allow them to eat almost anything. They can attack prey that is larger than they are. Bony fish, dolphins, stingrays, sea turtles, and other sharks are some of their favorite foods. Bull sharks that live in rivers have been known to feast on dogs, antelopes, and even young hippos!

Bull sharks often appear sluggish as they hunt. However, they can burst to speeds over 11 miles (18 kilometers) per hour. Bull sharks have small eyes and poor vision. They must use other senses to find food. A keen sense of smell allows them to sniff out prey. The ampullae of Lorenzini are tiny pores around the shark's snout. These sense the electric fields of nearby animals. The lateral lines on the sides of the body sense the movements of prey in the water.

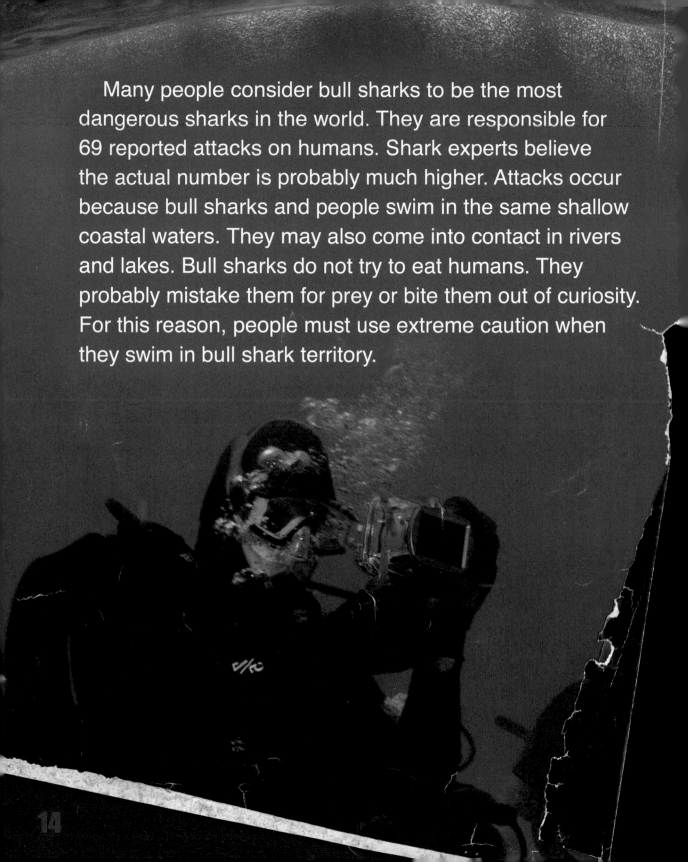

Many people consider bull sharks to be the most dangerous sharks in the world. They are responsible for 69 reported attacks on humans. Shark experts believe the actual number is probably much higher. Attacks occur because bull sharks and people swim in the same shallow coastal waters. They may also come into contact in rivers and lakes. Bull sharks do not try to eat humans. They probably mistake them for prey or bite them out of curiosity. For this reason, people must use extreme caution when they swim in bull shark territory.

Despite their fierce reputation, bull sharks can also be calm. Some people enjoy diving with bull sharks as they cruise along the sandy ocean floor. They must dive with experienced guides and follow strict guidelines to stay safe. What a thrill to swim among such massive fish!

HOLD THE SALT

Most sharks cannot survive outside of saltwater. Bull sharks can live in freshwater because they are able to maintain the right amount of salt in their bodies.

People all over the world hunt bull sharks for a variety of reasons. Sport fishers enjoy the challenge of catching these strong sharks on fishing lines. One of the largest bull sharks caught with a rod and reel weighed over 700 pounds (318 kilograms)!

Bull sharks are also fished for their meat. People buy it fresh, frozen, or smoked. Their fins are sold at a high price in Asian countries. People use them to make shark fin soup. Shark livers are taken for oil, and the skin is made into leather. Some people keep the bull shark's jaws as a trophy.

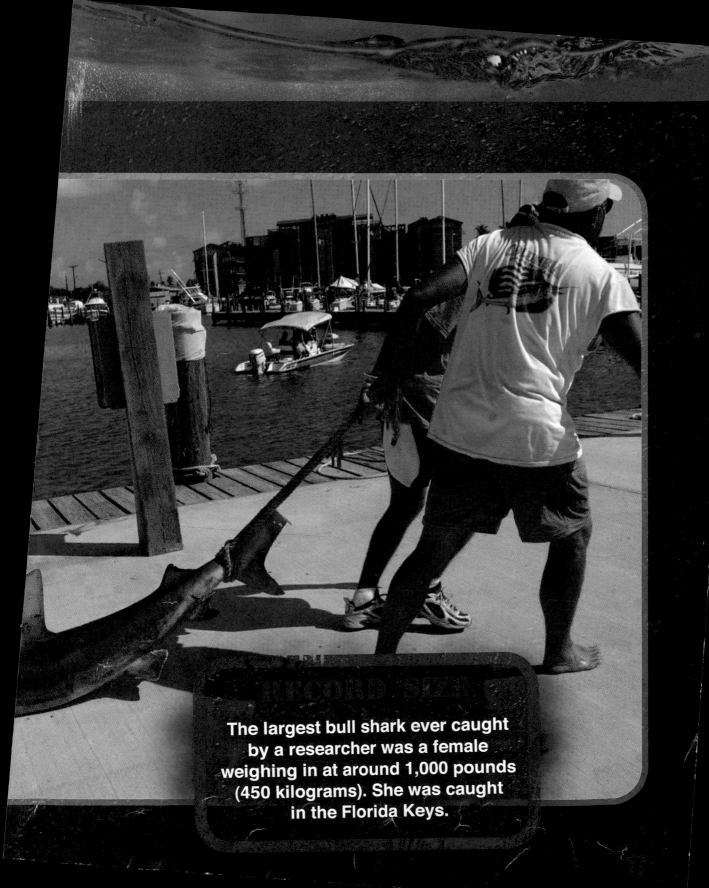

The largest bull shark ever caught by a researcher was a female weighing in at around 1,000 pounds (450 kilograms). She was caught in the Florida Keys.

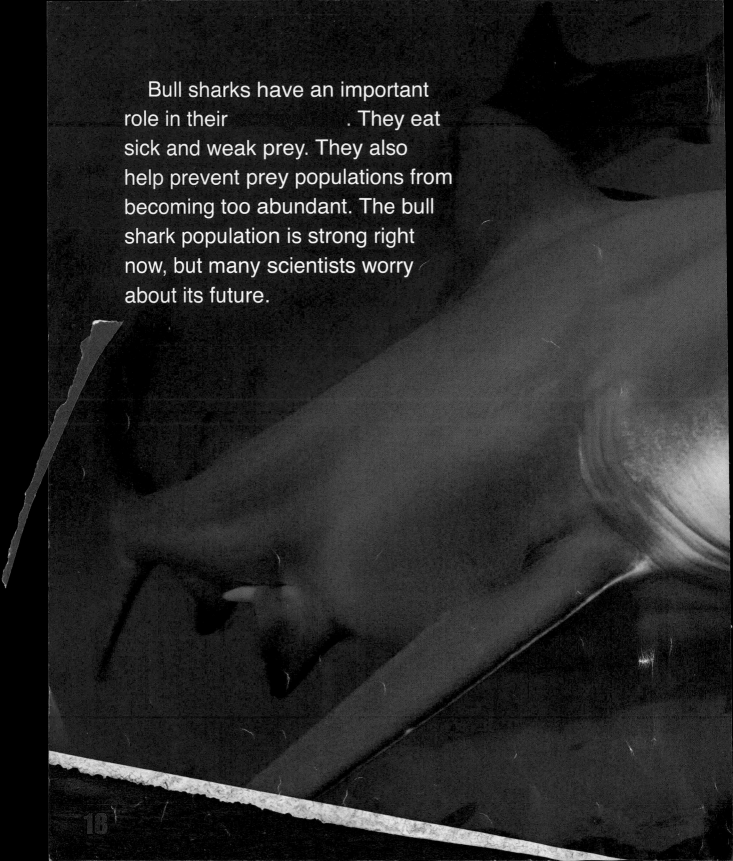

Bull sharks have an important role in their   . They eat sick and weak prey. They also help prevent prey populations from becoming too abundant. The bull shark population is strong right now, but many scientists worry about its future.

One of the greatest threats facing the bull shark is habitat destruction. Sharks need plenty of clean water to live and give birth to young. When humans pollute coastal waters, bull sharks suffer. Because of this, the bull shark has been listed as near threatened by the International Union for Conservation of Nature (IUCN).

Bull Shark

Nicaragua Shark
Zambezi Shark
River Shark

Swims into freshwater
rivers and lakes

Florida
Mexico
The Bahamas

12 to 16 years

Near Threatened (IUCN)

EXTINCT

EXTINCT IN
THE WILD

CRITICALLY
ENDANGERED

ENDANGERED

VULNERABLE

NEAR
THREATENED

LEAST
CONCERN

Scientists continue to learn more about bull sharks
every year. One way they gather information is by
following sharks as they migrate. To do this, they attach
an electronic tag to a shark's dorsal fin. The tag records
information about the shark's travel patterns.

Researchers use tagging to discover new places where bull sharks live and give birth. They use this information to educate others and make conservation plans. With the help of the public, this fearsome fish will continue to fascinate people for years to come!

GLOSSARY

ampullae of Lorenzini—a network of tiny jelly-filled sacs around a shark's snout; the jelly is sensitive to the electric fields of nearby prey.

apex predators—predators that are not hunted by any other animal

cartilage—flexible connective tissue that makes up a shark's skeleton

conservation—the protection and preservation of something

countershading—coloring that helps camouflage an animal; fish with countershading have pale bellies and dark backs.

dorsal fins—the fins on the back of a fish

ecosystem—a community of organisms and their environment

electric field—waves of electricity created by movement; every living being has an electric field.

estuaries—places where a river meets the ocean

freshwater—water that has little to no salt; lakes, ponds, rivers, and streams contain freshwater.

lateral line—a system of tubes beneath a shark's skin that helps it detect changes in water pressure

mature—to become old enough to reproduce

migrate—to travel from one place to another, often with the seasons

near threatened—could soon be at risk of becoming endangered

pectoral fins—a pair of fins that extend from each side of a fish's body

serrated—having a jagged edge

viviparous—producing young that develop inside the body; viviparous animals give birth to live young.

To Learn More

At the Library

Dubowski, Cathy East. *Shark Attack!* New York, N.Y.: Dorling Kindersley, 2009.

Gussoni, Clizia. *The Awesome Book of Sharks*. Philadelphia, Pa.: Running Press Kids, 2006.

Owings, Lisa. *Bull Shark Attack*. Minneapolis, Minn.: Bellwether Media, Inc., 2013.

On the Web

Learning more about bull sharks
is as easy as 1, 2, 3.

1. Go to www.factsurfer.com.

2. Enter "bull sharks" into the search box.

3. Click the "Surf" button and you will see a list
of related Web sites.

With factsurfer.com, finding more information
is just a click away.